MANON

Poëme de M.M.
H. MEILHAC et PH. GILLE

Musique de
J. MASSENET

Jules Massenet: *Manon* (1884). Poster by Antonin-Marie Chatinière.

LUCY BROIDO

FRENCH OPERA POSTERS 1868-1930

Dover Publications, Inc., New York

ACKNOWLEDGMENTS

I should like to thank François Heugel for his help and both Philippe and François Heugel for introducing me to this fascinating collection of posters.

Thanks are also due to the librarians of the Bibliothèque de l'Opéra and the Cabinet des Estampes of the Bibliothèque Nationale in Paris for their helpfulness and courtesy.

Published in Canada by General Publishing Company,
Ltd., 30 Lesmill Road, Don Mills, Toronto, Ontario.
Published in the United Kingdom by Constable and
Company, Ltd., 10 Orange Street, London WC 2.

French Opera Posters, 1868–1930 is a new work, first published
by Dover Publications, Inc., in 1976.

International Standard Book Number: 0-486-23306-5
Library of Congress Catalog Card Number: 75-32586

Manufactured in the United States of America
Dover Publications, Inc.
180 Varick Street
New York, N.Y. 10014

INTRODUCTION

The modern illustrated poster is barely more than a hundred years old. Although lithography was invented in 1798, it was only in the mid-nineteenth century that presses were developed which could produce large posters in quantity. In 1896 Ernest Maindron (*Les Affiches Illustrées*) marveled about the new developments:

> What would Aloys Senefelder, the glorious inventor of lithography, say; what would Godfrey Engelmann, the . . . creator of chromolithography, say . . . ? Surely the sight of these gigantic proofs, the joy of our eyes, would fill them with justifiable pride.

While large powerful presses made posters possible, it was the advent of mass production and the sudden need for mass advertising that made them necessary. The new department stores, bulging with wares, had to draw customers from all over the city, as did theaters, concert halls, large cafés and opera houses. Manufacturers strove to make the name of their product a household word and usually did it in the same way as today—with a picture of a provocative girl—whether selling perfume, ink, bicycles, lamp oil or mineral water.

Although late nineteenth-century Paris seethed with denunciations of avant-garde music, theater and art, there was almost universal pleasure at the gaiety which posters brought to the city streets. From the start, enthusiasts collected posters by buying them, bribing the men who put them up or by stealthily sponging them off the walls. Printers sometimes pulled examples in two formats, a large size for posting and a smaller size for the collector. Books were written about posters, exhibitions were held and reproductions were widely sold. Because posters did not call themselves art, because they could be enjoyed without the responsibility of judgment, they did (and still do) their part in bringing new artistic movements to a far larger public than ever visits museums. It is not a contradiction that since 1884 there have been poster exhibits, for although they are being looked at in a gallery, they are still being seen as posters and not asking for acceptance as great or serious art. Like popular songs, light theater and other people's children, they are enjoyed for the moment, ephemerally, needing no commitment for the future.

The last decades of the nineteenth century were typical of all artistic transition periods, including ours. The avant-garde in Paris irritated the establishment, not only with its art, literature, music and theater, but with its spill-over into dress and life styles. A poem started, "Is it a young man? Is it a woman?", a critic suggested that a statue by Rodin "should be cast in bronze and set up high so that future centuries will know to what degree of mental aberration we have come at the end of this century" and experimental theaters sometimes became fighting arenas as when the lead character in Alfred Jarry's *Ubu Roi* shouted a show-stopping obscenity (Nouveau Théâtre, 1896). To approve of anything new in the arts was to risk being called a snobbish intellectual, or worse, un-French.

The musical world of late nineteenth-century France was a battleground on which romanticism and *verismo* (realism) were only two of the opponents. Wagner, with his advanced harmonies and leitmotifs, was regarded with suspicion, derision and horror, and French composers were exhorted not to follow this madman. As usual, art and music strolled along together. While radical changes began to be felt in all of the arts, operas were still, for the most part, exotically set around myths, legends or love stories of the past, matching the Salon paintings whose plump pink and white nudes cavorted with cupids and gods in settings that never were.

The same time span, however, witnessed the golden age of the French operetta with the innovative works of Hervé, the superb creations of Offenbach and the charming contributions of the younger composers. French operetta moved rapidly from burlesques of serious operas through a wide range of subjects and styles, until, by the turn of the century, it was often quite close to musical comedy.

During this period, most of the ballets produced at the Paris Opéra were merely embroideries on the great Romantic achievements of the 1830s and 1840s. No basic innovations were in store until the impact of Diaghilev around 1910, but with its beautiful scores and brilliant choreographers and performers, French ballet remained an important part of the musical scene.

The 53 French posters represented here, dating from 1868 to 1930, were all commissioned by the Parisian music publishers Heugel & Cie and G. Hartmann and are part of my personal collection. They advertise 30 operas, 16 operettas, 6 ballets and one oratorio published by that firm. In most cases, the performances involved were world premières or at least first productions in France. Important composers and many still-performed works are included, and outstanding poster artists and print shops are represented.

The history of the Heugel firm goes back to the publishing house founded in 1812 by Jean-Antoine Meissonnier, whom Jacques-Léopold Heugel joined in 1839. When Heugel died in 1883, the greatest singers and composers took part in his funeral service, which was attended by 3000 people. The business is now managed by the great-grandsons of Jacques-Léopold: François-Henri and Philippe-Gérard-André Heugel. The firm acquired the valuable Hartmann catalogue in 1891 and the Tellier titles in 1898.

The Heugel list of publications includes works of the composers noted in this volume and, among others, Auric, Bizet, d'Indy, Honegger, Ibert, Lalo, Milhaud, Poulenc, Ravel, Taillefer and Tcherepnin. From 1833 to 1940 Heugel also published an important weekly magazine, *Le Ménestrel*, which dealt with music, literature, theater and fashion.

In a history of the firm written for the family archives, François Heugel describes the lively headquarters at 2 *bis*, Rue Vivienne, where such glamorous divas as Sybil Sanderson, Emma Calvé and Mary Garden would come to call, and where Massenet had an office for himself. Massenet said, speaking of Henri-Georges Heugel and his wife, that he "owed them everything, never having had any dissension with them whatever!" After 136 years on the Rue Vivienne, Heugel & Cie are now located in the gardens of the Palais-Royal.

BIBLIOGRAPHY

Standard reference works (biographical dictionaries, collections of opera plot summaries, etc.) are not included here.

Abdy, Jane, *The French Poster*, Studio Vista, London, 1969.

Anspach, Pierre A. L., *Les Cahiers du Théâtre de la Monnaie*, Brussels, Nos. 1–8, n.d.

Art du Théâtre, L'; Revue Mensuelle, Charles Schmid, Paris, 1903, 1904, 1906.

Barnicoat, John, *A Concise History of Posters 1870–1970*, Abrams, N.Y., 1972.

Bénézit, E., *Dictionnaire de Peintres, Sculpteurs, Dessinateurs et Graveurs*, Librairie Gründ, Paris, 1950.

Bibliothèque Nationale, Département des Estampes, Inventaire du Fonds Français, après 1800, Vols. I–XIV (Adhémar, Lethève, Gardey, Laran), Paris, 1930–1967.

Harding, James, *Massenet*, St. Martin's Press, N.Y., 1970.

Hillier, Bevis, *Posters*, Spring Books, London, 1969; Hamlyn, 1974.

Jullien, Adolphe, *Musiciens d'Aujourd'hui*, Librairie de l'Art, Paris, first series 1892, second series 1894.

Loewenberg, Alfred (ed.), *Annals of Opera 1597–1940*, Vol. I, Societas Bibliographica, Geneva, 2nd ed., 1955.

Lubbock, Mark, *The Complete Book of Light Opera*, Putnam, London, 1962.

Maindron, Ernest, *Les Affiches Illustrées*, G. Boudet, Paris, 1896.

Mallet, Dominique, *Albert Maignan et Son Oeuvre*, Mamers, 1913.

Man, Felix H., *Artist's Lithographs; A World History from Senefelder to the Present Day*, G. P. Putnam's Sons, N.Y., 1970.

Mémoires de l'Académie de Dijon 1899–1900, pp. 289–316, Henri Chabeuf.

Rudorff, Raymond, *The Belle Epoque; Paris in the Nineties*, Saturday Review Press, N.Y., 1973.

Scala, La; 400 Years of Stage Design, Museo Teatrale, La Scala, Milan, 1971.

Scène, La; Revue des Succès Dramatiques, Vol. I, Paris, 1877.

Schneider, Louis, *Massenet, l'Homme et le Musicien*, Librairie L. Conquet, Paris, 1908.

Stuart, Henry, *French Essays and Profiles*, E. P. Dutton & Co., N.Y., 1921.

Théâtre, Le; Revue Bimensuelle Illustrée, Goupil et Cie, Paris, various issues, 1897–1919.

Vaillat, Léandre, *Ballets de l'Opéra de Paris*, Compagnie Française des Arts Graphiques, Paris, 1943.

ALPHABETICAL LIST OF ARTISTS

Biographical information on the artists will be found in the Notes to the Plates. Where an artist is represented by more than one poster, this information is located in the note to the first of his posters that occurs.

THE PLATES

1. Rodolphe Berger: *Le Chevalier d'Eon* (1908). Poster by Clérice Frères.

3. Léo Delibes: *Jean de Nivelle* (1880). Poster by A. Barbizet.

4. Théodore Dubois: *La Farandole* (1884). Poster by Jules Chéret.

5. Théodore Dubois: *Aben-Hamet* (1884). Poster by Manuel Orazi.

6. Gabriel Dupont: *La Glu* (1910). Poster by Robert Dupont.

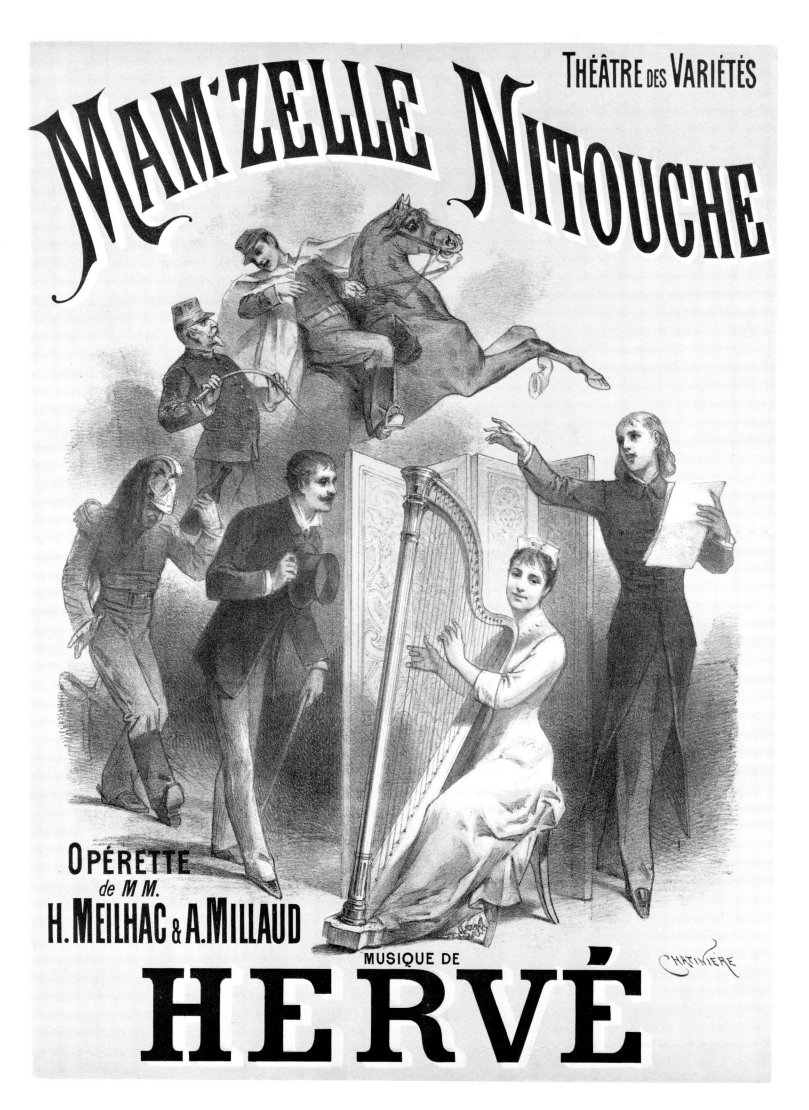

7. Hervé: *Mam'zelle Nitouche* (1883). Poster by Antonin-Marie Chatinière.

Au MÉNESTREL, 2 *bis*, rue Vivienne, Paris.

Pietro Mascagni
Chevalerie Rustique

DRAME LYRIQUE EN UN ACTE

de MM.

J. TARGIONI-TOZZETTI et G. MENASCI

version française de M. PAUL MILLIET

Réduction pour Chant et Piano . . . net Fr. **12** —
Réduction pour Piano . . . . » » **6** —

MORCEAUX SÉPARÉS:

Prix nets:

SICILIENNE . . . . Fr. 1 50	REFRAIN DE LOLA . . . . Fr. 2 —
ROMANCE ET SCÈNE . . . . » 2 —	BRINDISI DE TURIDDU. . . . . » 3 —
SCÈNE ET ENTRÉE D'ALFIO . . . . . . » 2 50	INTERMEZZO SINFONICO, Transcription pour Piano. . » 2 —

REDUCTIONS ET TRANSCRIPTIONS POUR INSTRUMENTS DIVERS:

Prix nets:

Azzoni I. . . . PETITE TRANSCRIPTION pour Piano . . Fr. 2 50
Celega N. . . FANTAISIE-TRANSCRIPTION pour Piano
à quatre mains . . . . » 4 50
De Simone C. SICILIENNE, Transcription facile pour Piano . » 2 —
— CHŒUR D'INTRODUCTION, Transcription
facile pour Piano . . . . » 3 50
— ROMANCE DE SANTUZZA, Transcription
facile pour Piano . . . . » 2 —

De Simone C. SCÈNE, CHŒUR ET CHANSON À
BOIRE, Transcription facile pour Piano . . Fr. 3 50
Fumagalli D.. TRANSCRIPTION pour Piano . . . . . » 4 —
— INTERMEZZO, Transcription pour Piano . . » 2 —
Menozzi J. . . FANTAISIE pour Piano . . . . » 3 50
Mugnone F. . . TRANSCRIPTION pour Violon avec accompa-
gnement de Piano . . . . » 4 —
Mugnone L. . MELODIES, Transcriptes pour Piano. . . . » 3 50

Prix marqués:

Anschütz I. A. BOUQUET DE MÉLODIES . . . . . Fr. 7 50
Bull G. . . . SILHOUETTE (N. 38) Fantaisie facile pour Piano » 5 —
Herman Ad. . FANTAISIE pour Violon et Piano . . . . Fr. 9 —
Neustedt Ch. FANTAISIE-TRANSCRIPTION pour Piano . » 7 50

Milan. — Imprimerie Edouard Sonzogno.

8. Pietro Mascagni: *Chevalerie Rustique* (1892). Anonymous artist.

THÉÂTRE NATIONAL DE L'OPÉRA-COMIQUE

PAUL & VIRGINIE

OPÉRA EN 3 ACTES
ET 6 TABLEAUX

DE
VICTOR MASSÉ

9. Victor Massé: *Paul et Virginie* (1876). Poster by Edward Ancourt.

FESTIVALS DE L'OPÉRA

MESDAMES
KRAUSS, DARAM
MESD.   M.M.
JANVIER BARBOT & LAURENT CARON

La Vierge

LÉGENDE SACRÉE
DE
CH·GRANDMOUGIN

MUSIQUE DE

J·MASSENET

PARIS G·HARTMANN·
60 Rue Nve St Augustin
Propriété pr tous pays

Imp. Fouquet, Paris.

10. Jules Massenet: *La Vierge* (1880). Anonymous artist.

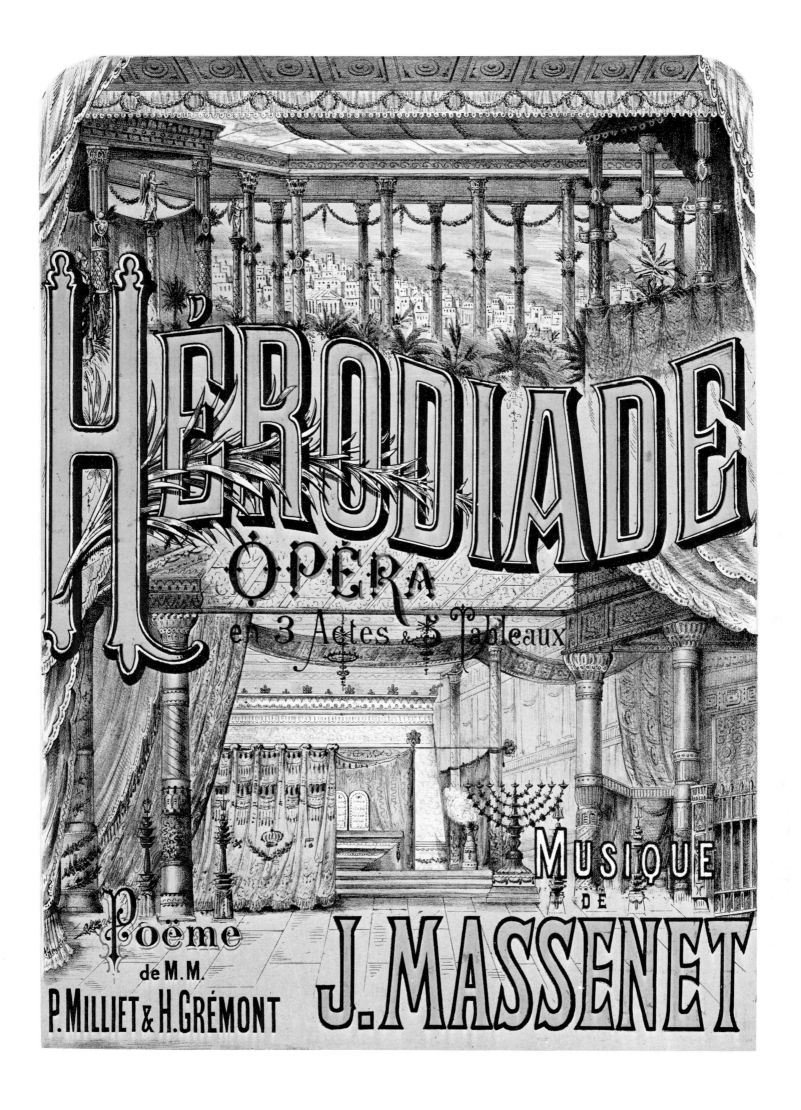

11. Jules Massenet: *Hérodiade* (1881). Poster by Charles Lévy.

12. Jules Massenet: *Le Cid* (1885). Poster by Georges Clairin.

THÉÂTRE NATIONAL DE L'OPÉRA-COMIQUE

LA NAVARRAISE

Épisode Lyrique en 2 Actes
de
JULES CLARETIE & HENRI CAIN
Musique de
J. MASSENET

Reutlinger phot.

Imp. Berthaud, 9 Rue Cadet, Paris

Paris – Au Ménestrel, 2 bis Rue Vivienne, HEUGEL & Cie Editeurs.

13. Jules Massenet: *La Navarraise* (1895). Photo by Reutlinger.

14. Jules Massenet: *Roma* (1912). Poster by Georges Rochegrosse.

L'OCA DEL CAIRO

COMPOSÉ
A
VIENNE
(1783)

PUBLIÉ
EN
ALLEMAGNE
(1861)

L'OIE
DU
CAIRE

Opéra-Bouffe inédit en DEUX actes

REPRÉSENTÉ A PARIS, AU **THÉATRE DES FANTAISIES PARISIENNES**, LE 6 JUIN 1867

POËME
DE
Victor WILDER

PARTITION
POUR
Piano et CHANT

ŒUVRE POSTHUME
DE
MOZART

HEUGEL et Cⁱᵉ, Éditeurs

Paris. — Typographie Morris et Comp., rue Amelot, 64.

EN VENTE ICI : Partition Piano et Chant, Piano solo, Morceaux détachés, Transcriptions et Arrangements.

15. Wolfgang Amadeus Mozart: *L'Oie du Caire* (ca. 1868). Illustration by Stop.

16. Jacques Offenbach: *Le Château à Toto* (1868). Poster by Jules Chéret.

17. Manuel Rosenthal: *Rayon des Soieries* (1930). Poster by Maurice Dufrène.

18. Ambroise Thomas: *Psyché* (1878). Illustration by Antonin-Marie Chatinière.

19. Ambroise Thomas: *La Tempète* (1889). Poster by E. Buval with illustration by Bellenger.

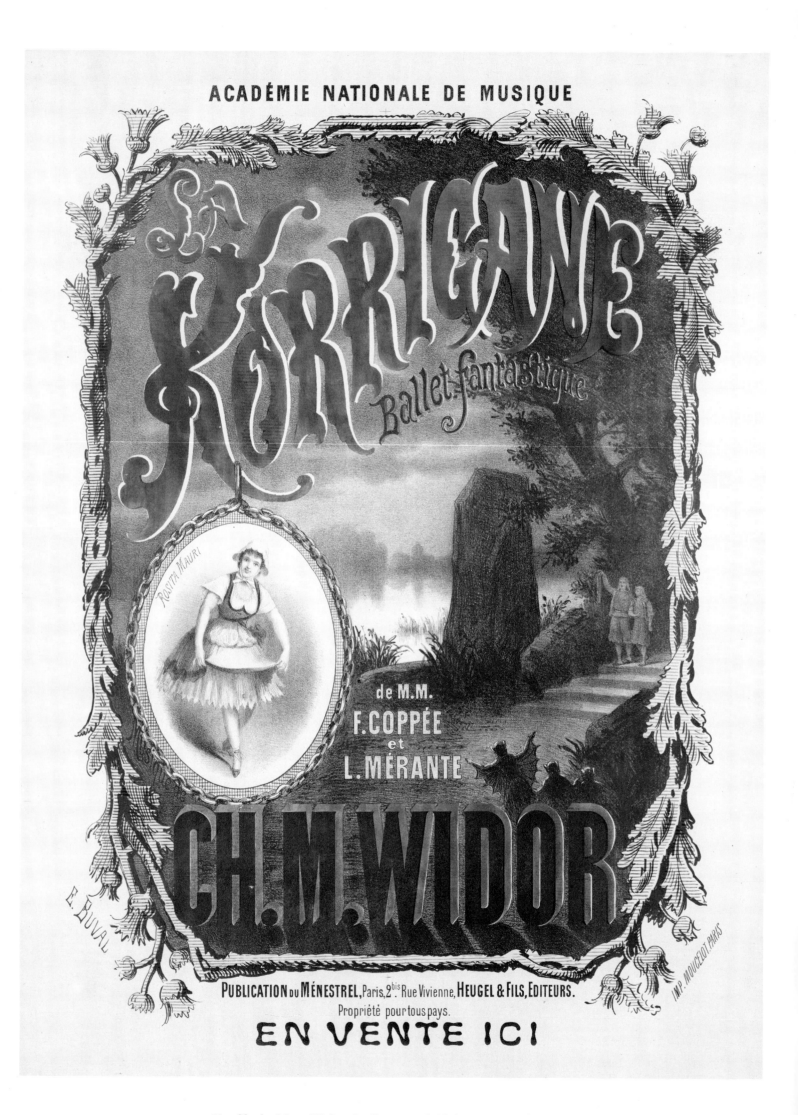

20. Charles-Marie Widor: *La Korrigane* (1880). Poster by E. Buval.

21. Rodolphe Berger: *Claudine* (1910). Poster by Clérice Frères.

22. Gustave Charpentier: *Louise* (1900). Poster by Georges Rochegrosse.

23. Gabriel Dupont: *Antar* (1921). Poster by Georges Rochegrosse.

24. Gabriel Fauré: *Pénélope* (1913). Poster by Georges Rochegrosse.

25. Henri Février: *Monna Vanna* (1909). Poster by Gustave Fraipont.

26. Henri Février: *Carmosine* (1913). Poster by Vikke van den Bergh.

27. Henri Février: *Gismonda* (1919). Poster by Georges Rochegrosse.

28. Léon Gastinel: *Le Rêve* (1890). Poster by Théophile-Alexandre Steinlen.

29. Gustave Goublier: *Mam'zelle Boy-Scout* (1915). Poster by Henri Gray.

30. Hervé: *Les Turcs* (1869). Poster by Jules Chéret.

31. Jules Massenet: *Esclarmonde* (1889). Poster by Alfred Choubrac.

32. Jules Massenet: *Le Mage* (1891). Poster by Alfredo Edel.

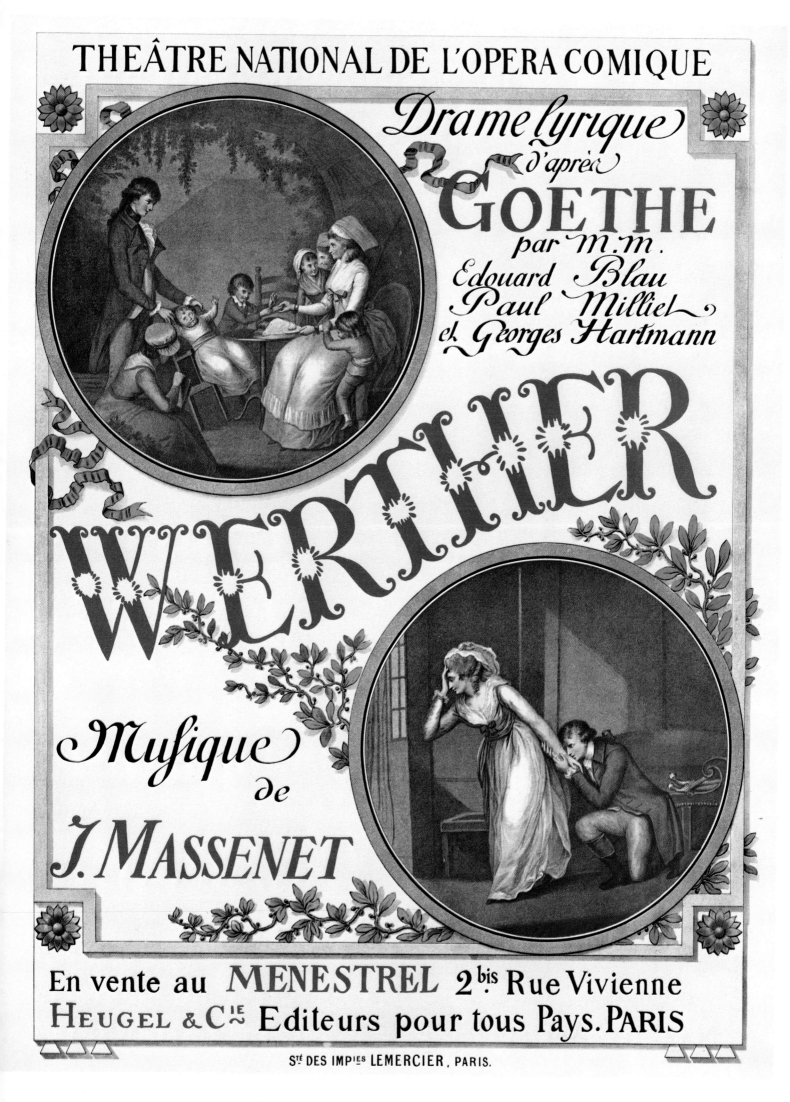

33. Jules Massenet: *Werther* (1893). Poster by Eugène Grasset.

34. Jules Massenet: *Thaïs* (1894). Poster by Manuel Orazi.

35. Jules Massenet: *Cendrillon* (1899). Poster by Emile Bertrand.

36. Jules Massenet: *Grisélidis* (1901). Poster by François Flameng.

37. Jules Massenet: *Cigale* (1904). Poster by Maurice Leloir.

38. Jules Massenet: *Le Jongleur de Notre-Dame* (1904). Poster by Georges Rochegrosse.

THÉÂTRE NATIONAL DE L'OPÉRA-COMIQUE

CHÉRUBIN

COMÉDIE CHANTÉE EN 3 ACTES

DE MRS FRANCIS DE CROISSET & HENRI CAIN

MUSIQUE DE J. MASSENET

Maurice Leloir

DEVAMBEZ. GRAV. PARIS.

39. Jules Massenet: *Chérubin* (1905). Poster by Maurice Leloir.

40. Jules Massenet: *Ariane* (1906). Poster by Albert Maignan.

41.   Jules Massenet: *Don Quichotte* (1910). Poster by Georges Rochegrosse.

Panurge

Haulte Farce Musicale en 3 Actes de M.M.
Georges Spitzmuller
et Maurice Boukay

Massenet

42. Jules Massenet: *Panurge* (1913). Poster by Charles-Lucien Léandre.

44. Victor Roger: *Les Fêtards* (1897). Poster after Pal.

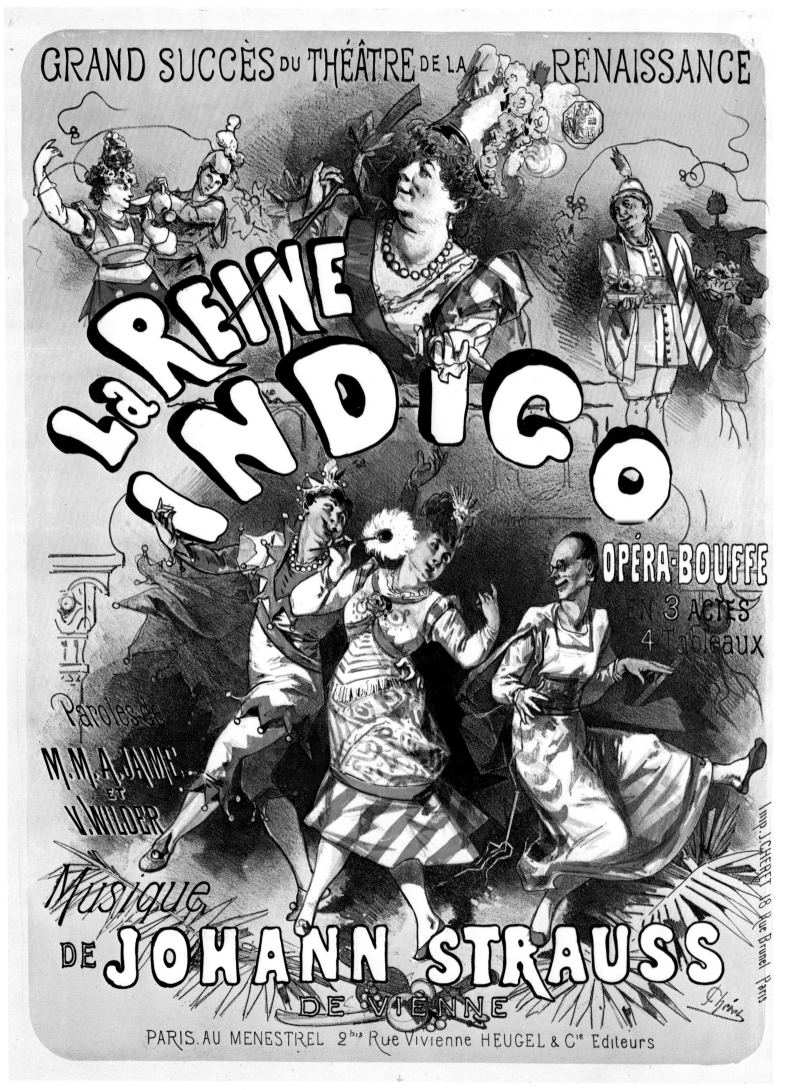

45. Johann Strauss II: *La Reine Indigo* (1875). Poster by Jules Chéret.

46. Johann Strauss II: *La Tzigane* (1877). Poster by Jules Chéret.

47. Johann Strauss II: *La Chauve-Souris* (1904). Poster by Georges Dola.

48. Ambroise Thomas: *Françoise de Rimini* (1882). Poster by Jules Chéret.

49. Louis Varney: *Le Papa de Francine* (1896). Poster by Alfred Choubrac (?).

50. Louis Varney: *Les Demoiselles des Saint-Cyriens* (1898). Poster by Jacques Wély.

51. Louis Varney: *Le Fiancé de Thylda* (1900). Poster by René Péan.

52. Charles-Marie Widor: *Les Pêcheurs de Saint-Jean* (1906). Poster by Fernand-Louis Gottlob.

NOTES TO THE PLATES

NOTES TO THE PLATES

The posters in the present volume are arranged alphabetically by composers and chronologically within one composer's work—with a separate listing in the black-and-white and in the color section. The captions on the picture pages give the name of the composer, the name of the work, the year of the poster and the name of the artist. Fuller information, including brief biographies of composers and artists, plot summaries, premières, printers and other background data, will be found in the following Notes. The Bibliography will be found after the Notes.

All the posters are color lithographs printed in Paris unless otherwise noted. The dimensions are given in inches, height before width. With rare noted exceptions, each poster announces the first performance of the work. The theater and date of each world première are given after the name of the composer; where no city is mentioned, Paris is understood.

Frontispiece: MANON. Opera; text by Henri Meilhac and Philippe Gille; music by Jules Massenet (1842–1912). Opéra-Comique, Jan. 19, 1884.

Poster by Antonin-Marie Chatinière; 35½ x 25; printed by E. Delanchy.

Chatinière, a painter and lithographer (born 1828), exhibited at the Salon de Paris in 1859, 1861 and 1867. He was so much in demand as a designer of music covers that his friends had to help him fill orders.

It is fitting that Massenet dominates this collection (he is also represented by Nos. 10–14 and 31–42), since he was the leading French opera composer of the time. He cheerfully worked like a galley slave, rising at four in the morning and often putting in a 16-hour day. He involved himself in every aspect of production, not always without unpleasant conflicts, but had the reward of remaining in vogue throughout a 45-year career.

Manon was Massenet's greatest success and by 1955 had had almost 2000 performances at the Opéra-Comique alone. Massenet composed the music in The Hague, in the same house that Prévost had lived in while writing the famous novel on which the opera is based. Sybil Sanderson made her American debut in the title role at the Metropolitan's first performance in 1895.

The immediate critical acceptance of *Manon* was by no means unanimous. In *Le Radical*, Henry Maret berated Massenet for not having understood, if indeed he had ever read, Prévost's novel: "From this simple and graceful pastel, he has made a frightful fresco . . . the light and elegant Manon becomes a Walkyrie."

The poster, a black-and-white lithograph, shows the end of the opera (Act V), a lonely road near Le Havre, with the faithful des Grieux grieving at the death of his beloved Manon. The two lovers had been separated first by his father's disapproval, and then by Manon's own capricious, pleasure-seeking behavior, which, in the end, brought her to prison and death.

1. LE CHEVALIER D'EON. Operetta; text by Armand Silvestre and Henri Cain; music by Rodolphe Berger (d. 1916). Théâtre de la Porte-Saint-Martin, Apr. 10, 1908.

Poster by Clérice Frères; 35½ x 25½; printed by Delanchy.

The poster studio of the Brothers Clérice on the Faubourg Poissonnière turned out a good many of their own designs.

Berger was a Viennese composer of operettas and waltzes, fashionable in turn-of-the-century Paris. During World War I, he had to leave his beloved France as an enemy alien. He moved to Spain, close to the French border, but died before he could return to Paris. See also No. 21.

The Chevalier d'Eon (the character is based on a real eighteenth-century diplomat) is sent to the court of Catherine the Great as an ambassadress: he must wear women's clothing in his official appearances.

This poster has red letters and figures in green, blue, red and gold on a gold and white background.

2. LES CHARBONNIERS (The Coal Dealers). Operetta; text by Philippe Gille; music by Jules Costé (d. 1901). Théâtre des Variétés, Apr. 4, 1877.

Poster with illustrations by Frédéric Régamey; 14¾ x 22; illustrations printed by Michelet; poster printed by the Imprimerie Centrale des Chemins de Fer and A. Chaix et Cⁱᵉ.

Régamey (1849–1925) was a painter, engraver and lithographer.

Adolphe Dupuis (left-hand illustration), a high tenor, was a leading star of French operetta, having created the male leads in Offenbach's *La Belle Hélène* and *La Grande Duchesse de Gérolstein.* The career of Anna Judic started somewhat later, but was also illustrious. The verse on the left says: "What a hulk of a man! Any scrape with him would give you the jitters. If you came to grips with him, you could never get off undamaged!" And on the right: "Washing up on Sundays, what a darn shame! A little black on your mug makes your white teeth stand out so prettily!"

In this one-act operetta, a male and female coal dealer who do not get along with each other change their minds and fall in love after they have had a good wash.

The illustrations in black portraying Dupuis and Judic were taken from the collection of *L'Eclipse*. The poster itself, in blue letters on lighter blue paper, was used on the railroad to advertise publications from the operetta.

3. JEAN DE NIVELLE. Opera; text by Edmond Gondinet and Philippe Gille; music by Léo Delibes (1836–1891). Opéra-Comique, March 8, 1880.
Poster by A. Barbizet; 32 x 22½; printed by Moucelot.

Barbizet was an artist and lithographer much in demand by music publishers for his ornamental lettering and designs for title pages. He did many theater posters between 1863 and 1880, sometimes signing with the first initial "J."

The theater works by Delibes that still hold the boards are his ballets *Coppélia* (1870) and *Sylvia* (1876) and his opera *Lakmé* (1883).

The nobleman Jean de Montmorency, banished by Louis XI for not marrying the woman chosen for him by the king, goes to the independent duchy of Burgundy disguised as a shepherd, Jean de Nivelle.

In an unflattering review in *Le Théâtre*, Adolphe Jullien calls this a grand opera without recitative and an *opéra comique* without the *comique*. He finds all French composers except Gounod lacking in originality. After intimating that Gondinet had given the *Jean de Nivelle* libretto to Delibes to undo the damage done by his previous *Le Roi l'a Dit*, Jullien asks: "Now that M. Delibes has set both, what libretto is M. Gondinet going to offer to undo the damage of *Le Roi l'a Dit* AND *Jean de Nivelle*?"

The title of the poster is in the medium green of the background; the other letters are brown. The banner is white, with gold cord and fringe.

4. LA FARANDOLE. Ballet; scenario by Philippe Gille, Arnold Mortier and Louis Mérante; music by Théodore Dubois (1837–1924). Opéra, Dec. 14, 1883.
Poster, 1884, by Jules Chéret; 28¼ x 21½; printed by the Chéret branch of Chaix.

Chéret, acknowledged as the father of the modern poster, was born in Paris in 1836, the son of a lithographer. At 14, he started working in a lithographic shop and stayed four years doing letters and drawings for advertisements. From 1855 to 1857 he did about 15 posters advertising novels and in 1858 he produced the poster for *Orphée aux Enfers* in orange, green and black, marking the real beginning of the modern illustrated poster. In 1859 he went to London to further his study of color lithography. There the famous perfumer Eugene Rimmel commissioned posters from Chéret and helped him gain the capital to launch his career. On Chéret's return to Paris in 1866, he opened his first print shop. His poster for *La Biche au Bois* created an immediate sensation and he was compared to Tiepolo, Watteau and Fragonard. In 1881 he transferred his printing operation to the firm of Chaix et Cie, retaining the position of artistic director. Thus for nine years his posters bore the imprint "Imprimerie Chaix (succursale Chéret)," *succursale* meaning branch, until in 1890 the two branches reunited at rue Bergère. In 1889 he had a one-man show of his pastels, lithographs, drawings, sketches for posters and the posters themselves, after which he was made a Chevalier of the Legion of Honor, an award previously conferred on only the most conservative established painters. There are no Chéret posters in this book

that are dated after 1886, but he went on producing them until 1900. He then went to Nice and painted until, like Degas, who had called him "the Watteau of the street," he went blind. He died in Nice in 1932. The Musée Chéret in that city contains hundreds of his works in all media, and some of his paintings hang in the Hermitage in Leningrad. A man of great charm, Chéret was loved not only by his many friends, but by the entire city of Paris. "I have always wanted to be pleasant," he said. "I find that life is sad often enough; I have known sadness, but I don't want to paint it."

Dubois, who won the Prix de Rome in 1861, was a leading composer, organist and music educator. Louis Mérante (1828–1887), who was part author of the scenario of *La Farandole*, also did the choreography and danced the chief male role, Olivier. He was the original choreographer and male lead of *Sylvia*, *La Korrigane* (see No. 20) and other notable Opéra ballets. The role of Vivette was danced by the great Rosita Mauri (see No. 19).

La Farandole, which takes place at Arles, is full of Provençal local color. Young Olivier is far too poor and shy to ask the hand of his beloved Vivette in marriage. When he and Vivette save the mysterious beggar Maurias from a beating, Maurias in gratitude tells Olivier how to win a rich reward: by visiting the ruins of the Roman amphitheater at midnight and resisting the temptations of the ghosts of beautiful girls who died for love of dancing. Olivier resists stoutly until Cigalia, the leader of these spirits, assumes the form of Vivette. While a diabolical farandole (chain dance) winds around him, he gives a wedding ring to the false Vivette. The next day, the real Vivette forgives him and is ready to marry him, when Cigalia arrives in a storm with her cohorts and claims him. But Maurias taps out the irresistible farandole on his Provençal drum and draws the lost souls after him into the abyss.

In the poster, the wicked sirens in the amphitheater (Act II) manage to look as delightfully pert as all of Chéret's girls. The small scene at lower right depicts an episode in Act I, when Vivette's girl friends give Olivier a lesson on how to approach Vivette's father and ask for her hand. At the bottom center is the Provençal drum (*tambourin*). The figures on the poster are in black and white on a pale green ground, with lettering in black.

5. ABEN-HAMET. Opera; text by Léonce Détroyat and A. Lauzières; music by Théodore Dubois. Théâtre-Italien-Châtelet, Dec. 16, 1884.
Poster by Manuel Orazi; 31½ x 23¾; printed by Delanchy & Cie.

Orazi, who was active between 1880 and 1905, often designed posters jointly with the artist Gorguet. He was also a jewelry designer.

The opera was performed in Italian by a private troupe. The company was directed by the great baritone Victor Maurel (the original Iago in Verdi's *Otello* and the original Falstaff), who sang the title role. The illustrious cast also included Edouard de Reszke and Emma Calvé.

Aben-Hamet, the son of Boabdil, the last Moorish king of Granada, visits Spain incognito to try to restore the fortunes of his dynasty, but while there falls in love with the daughter of the Spanish governor of Granada.

Adolphe Jullien, reviewing the opera for *Le Théâtre*, called it the composer's first great lyric work, but bemoaned the fact that Dubois had to give 12,000 francs to the Italian consulate "so that these Italian choruses, wicked as the Normans that they are, consent to sing the opera of a French composer in place of *Il Trovatore* and *La Traviata*." He adds that they sang off key for the money. The *Annals of Opera* reports that this was the last time that an original production of an opera with

Italian text was done in Paris. (The French version was done at Liège in 1885.)

This poster appears in *Les Affiches Illustrées*. The figure in the center is deep tan, brown and white; the letters are a rich orange-red and the notes are black.

6. LA GLU. Opera; text by Jean Richepin and Henri Cain; music by Gabriel Dupont (1878–1914). Nice, Jan. 24, 1910.

Poster by Robert Dupont (b. 1874); 35 x 25¾; printed by Delanchy.

The artist's monogram has been read as AR, CR and OR, but it may be an R with a reversed D, since Heugel's catalogue lists the artist as Robert Dupont. They suggest he was the composer's brother, a logical assumption since both were born in Caen, four years apart. Robert Dupont was a pupil of Delaunay and Moreau.

Gabriel Dupont, a pupil of Widor and Massenet, wrote several instrumental works and operas (see also No. 23). The noted poet Richepin was co-author of the libretto of *La Glu*, based on his own novel (1881) and play (1883) of the same name.

The poster illustrates a dramatic moment of Act I, Scene 2: the young Breton fisherman Marie-Pierre is discovered in the company of the Parisian adventuress La Glu by his widowed mother Marie-des-Anges, whom he has been neglecting in his state of infatuation. In the background, banjo on his shoulder, is the retired seaman Gillioury, whose song has decoyed the guilty couple out onto the balcony.

The figures and background are in black and a pale green, the lantern and the light behind the door are a glowing gold, and the lettering is white and a green-black mixture. As is still done now, posters were sometimes pulled with a blank space to be filled in later with the name of the theater; the letters at the top are in an unrelated style and color (blue).

7. MAM'ZELLE NITOUCHE (Miss Hypocrite). Operetta; text by Henri Meilhac and A. Millaud; music by Hervé (1825–1892). Théâtre des Variétés, Jan. 16, 1883.

Poster by Antonin-Marie Chatinière; 31 x 23½; printer unknown.

Hervé, whose real name was Florimond Ronger, was known as "the crazy composer," which is also the title of one of his many shows. He started by writing dramatic pieces for the lunatic asylum at which his mother worked, and later became a theater manager, actor, organist, singer, conductor, librettist and composer of numerous operettas, songs and ballets. He is generally credited as the creator of French operetta, having preceded Offenbach in this field. His masterpiece, *Mam'zelle Nitouche*, written specially for Judic (see No. 2), is still performed today. The role of Célestin reflects certain features of Hervé's own life. See also No. 30.

Célestin, proper organist at a provincial convent, is leading a second life as Floridor, the composer of a saucy operetta, about to be given its first performance in the municipal theater. Denise, a seemingly pious but really mischievous convent pupil, whom Célestin dubs "Mam'zelle Nitouche," knows his secret and has memorized his operetta. She winds up at the theater herself and goes on in place of the irate primadonna. Further adventures of Célestin and Denise that night include an uproarious party at the cavalry barracks.

The poster, black and white on a cream ground, shows the cavalry commandant, the drunken corporal of the guard at the barracks, Denise's young fiancé interviewing her at the convent with a screen between them, and finally Célestin.

8. CHEVALERIE RUSTIQUE (Cavalleria Rusticana). Opera; Italian text by J. Targioni-Tozzetti and G. Menasci (French text by Paul Milliet); music by Pietro Mascagni (1863–1945). Teatro Costanzi, Rome, May 17, 1890.

Anonymous poster, ca. 1892; 30 x 21½; printed by Edoardo Sonzogno, Milan.

Mascagni's well-known *Cavalleria Rusticana*, about love and revenge in a Sicilian village, was based on a contemporary short story and play by Giovanni Verga. It won a competition instituted by the publisher Sonzogno and catapulted its unknown composer into fame, although some of the audience at the première were "enraged, shouting and gesticulating," and there were those who accused Mascagni of money-grubbing and dubbed Sonzogno a "Barnum" (Anspach). The first Paris performance, at the Opéra-Comique in 1892, starred Emma Calvé as Santuzza (she made her Metropolitan Opera debut in that role the following year). There was a little booing in Paris, too, probably more because of political passions than from reaction against the work itself.

The main alteration made in the French version is at the end of the opera, where there is no duel between Alfio and Turiddu.

The lettering on the poster is dark brown, the white hawthorn (the first line of the opera is "O Lola, white as the hawthorn flower") rests on an earth color, and the background is cream-colored.

9. PAUL ET VIRGINIE. Opera; text by Jules Barbier and Michel Carré; music by Victor Massé (1822–1884). Opéra, Nov. 15, 1876.

Poster by Edward Ancourt; 25¼ x 35; probably printed by Ancourt.

The Toulouse-Lautrec cover for *L'Estampe Originale* shows Jane Avril in a print shop examining a lithograph just off the press. The shop is Ancourt's and the man at the press his master printer, Le Père Cotelle. Ancourt was a pioneer in color lithography and his shop was favored by Toulouse-Lautrec, Bonnard and a great many other artists. An artist himself, he did numerous posters between 1872 and 1887, including 23 for the theater. This one, in black and white, shows an early scene from the opera.

This was at least the third French opera based on the 1788 novel by Jacques-Henri Bernardin de Saint-Pierre. Massé, a pupil of Halévy and winner of the Prix de Rome in 1844, wrote several other operas.

The idyllic existence of the childhood sweethearts Paul and Virginie on a French-colonized island near Africa is brought to a jarring end when the girl is sent home to France. Her ship is wrecked in a terrible storm, and her body is washed ashore at Paul's feet.

In his review, Adolphe Jullien praises the librettists for closer adherence to the original story than their predecessors; about the music he comments: "M. Massé was obviously trying to combine his old manner, his more or less original melodies, always easy and pleasing to the public, with the new, somewhat worrisome ideas that he sees around him."

10. LA VIERGE (The Virgin). Oratorio; text by Ch. Grandmougin; music by Jules Massenet. Opéra, May 22, 1880.

Anonymous poster; 27½ x 21; printed by Fouquet.

On Massenet, see note on Frontispiece. See also Nos. 11–14 and 31–42. Unlike Massenet's earlier oratorios *Marie-Magdeleine* and *Eve*, *La Vierge* was unsuccessful, though it received later critical recognition. With the composer conducting, it was the first and last presentation in a projected series of Concerts Historiques at the Opéra.

The larger letters on the poster are dark blue with white highlights (like the flowers), while the smaller letters are dark green. The ground is a medium blue-green.

Note the Hartmann imprint as publisher of the music; Heugel acquired the Hartmann catalogue in 1891.

11. HÉRODIADE (Herodias). Opera; text by Paul Milliet and Henri Grémont (Georges Hartmann); music by Jules Massenet. Théâtre de la Monnaie, Brussels, Dec. 19, 1881.
Poster, 1881, by Charles Lévy; 28¼ x 22; printed by Lévy.

Charles Lévy was primarily a lithographic printer, but he was also an artist. Some of his studio's posters, like this one, bear the label "Affiches Américaines." Most of them deal with the café-concert world from 1878 to the end of the century.

Originally suggested by Ricordi in Milan, and scheduled for production at the Opéra in 1881 (the director reneged on grounds that the plot was "incendiary"), *Hérodiade*, the earliest Massenet opera still performed with some frequency, had its première in Brussels. It was coolly received in Paris three years later, and was not successful in that city until its 1903 revival with Emma Calvé. The title was changed to *Salomé* for the Covent Garden production in 1904. The librettist Milliet was a young and poor music student who was stunned at receiving the assignment from Massenet.

In this version of the Salome/John the Baptist story, Salome loves John sincerely and is willing to die with him. She directs her anger toward Herod, who desires her, and toward Herodias, whom she tries to kill for having caused John's death. On learning that Herodias is actually her mother, she kills herself instead.

In his review of the 1903 production, Louis Schneider defends the plot: "Biblical exactitude has nothing to do with the matter. The only concern a librettist must have is to furnish a composer with musical situations."

Most of the poster is a soft, transparent green, with touches of brown and lettering in red.

12. LE CID. Opera; text by Adolphe D'Ennery, Louis Gallet and Edouard Blau; music by Jules Massenet. Opéra, Nov. 30, 1885.
Poster by Georges Clairin; 28½ x 21½; printed by Lemercier & Cⁱᵉ.

Clairin (1843–1919), a student of Pils at the Beaux-Arts, did murals for public buildings and completed the work for the Paris Opéra that Pils could not finish. He also "made his name as a theatrical portraitist as well as a history painter, and for a long time was a close friend of Sarah Bernhardt, whom he painted in her many roles" (Rudorff).

This opera is based closely on the well-known seventeenth-century play by Pierre Corneille, in which an insult to family honor temporarily keeps apart the great Spanish champion and his sweetheart Chimène.

The reviews were mixed. "The score . . . stands out on the horizon of the contemporary school like an imposing peak colored with flames—those of the dawn or sunset? I haven't decided" (Auguste Vitu, *Le Figaro*). "The young chief of the old school . . . throws himself at the difficulties of the opera and lyric drama without benefiting one or the other" (Fourcaud, *Le Gaulois*). "Charm your ears with the inspired melodies" (Ernest Reyer, *Les Débuts*).

On the poster, the girl's figure is in pink, the large letters are red and the small ones black, as are the other figures. The background is tan.

13. LA NAVARRAISE (The Girl of Navarre). Opera; text by Jules Claretie and Henri Cain; music by Jules Massenet. Covent Garden, London, June 20, 1894.
Poster, 1895, with Reutlinger photo; 32½ x 24; printed by Berthaud.

Reutlinger was a busy turn-of-the-century photographer, specializing in women's portraits. The Print Room at the Bibliothèque Nationale has fifteen collections of his work, but no first name or dates for him.

La Navarraise, Massenet's contribution to the contemporary *verismo* movement in opera, was not performed in Paris until 1895, when this poster was prepared.

The heroine is a poor Basque girl who, in order to acquire a dowry, assassinates a rebel leader on whose head the Spanish government has placed a price. But her feat brings about the death of the man she loves, and she goes mad.

The striking *Navarraise* poster, prophetic of much later trends, was one of the few in the nineteenth century to use photographs. It shows Emma Calvé, who created the title role. The title and composer's name are in a rich blue and the other letters are black, all on a cream ground.

14. ROMA. Opera; text by Henri Cain; music by Jules Massenet. Monte Carlo, Feb. 17, 1912.
Poster by Georges Rochegrosse; 35¼ x 26¾; printed by Ed. Delanchy & Fils.

Rochegrosse (1859–1938), a pupil of Boulanger, did a great many official portraits and historical paintings, as well as magazine illustrations (*La Vie Parisienne*) and engravings for books. He was a man of his time, one of the establishment, whose paintings brought large prices from a French public who loved his subjects and admired his technique. Raymond Rudorff, in *The Belle Epoque*, states that Rochegrosse "was to painting what Cecil B. DeMille was to costume films . . . and he was a popular favorite until the early years of this century."

Roma, the last of Massenet's operas produced in his lifetime (he died August 13, 1912), was a huge success (the Paris première was April 24, 1912). Based on the play *Rome Vaincue* (1876) by Alexandre Parodi, in which Sarah Bernhardt starred, it is about a Vestal Virgin named Fausta who, as punishment for a forbidden love affair with the officer Lentulus, is sentenced to be walled up alive. Lucien Muratore was the original Lentulus in Paris, Marcel Journet was the Pontifex Maximus, and Lucy Arbell (see No. 41) was the blind grandmother Posthumia (the Bernhardt role in the play).

The poster shows Posthumia preparing to stab Fausta as an act of mercy. The grandmother is robed in a plum color, repeated in the young man's tunic. The rest of the scene is in gray and a rich dark blue, with all the letters in a medium blue.

15. L'OIE DU CAIRE (L'Oca del Cairo; The Cairo Goose). Opéra bouffe; French text by Victor Wilder; music compiled from works by Wolfgang Amadeus Mozart (1756–1791). Théâtre des Fantaisies Parisiennes, June 6, 1867.
Poster, ca. 1868, with illustrations by Stop (Louis Morel-Retz); 25½ x 20; type printed by Morris et Comp., illustration printed by Bertauts.

Morel-Retz (1825–1899) worked for the magazine *L'Illustration*, where he first used the pseudonym "Stop," the name of his dog. He also did comic and light political vignettes for *Charivari* and *Le Journal pour Rire*, and illustrated two volumes of his own poems, *Bêtes et Gens* (1877).

To call this a posthumous work (see poster) does not really state the case. Mozart never finished *L'Oca del Cairo* (1783) because he did not like Giambattista Varesco's text. Eight pieces from the first act were published in 1855. These, plus parts from another unfinished Mozart opera of 1783, *Lo Sposo Deluso*, and Mozart's additions to Bianchi's *La Villanella Rapita*, were arranged by T. C. Constantin for the Paris production, with a new French libretto by Wilder. The poster also mentions an 1861 German publication of the music.

The artificial goose of the title, pictured on the poster, conceals two young men, who thus gain entrance to a tower and win their brides.

The main body of the poster was printed in red letters on tan, with a white oval left blank. It then went to the Bertauts shop, where the black-and-white lithograph was printed on. This is probably the earliest poster in this volume.

16. LE CHÂTEAU À TOTO. Operetta; text by Henri Meilhac and Louis Halévy; music by Jacques Offenbach (1819–1880). Théâtre du Palais-Royal, May 6, 1868.
Poster by Jules Chéret; 29½ x 22; printed by Chéret.

Like many Parisians of the period, Chéret moved frequently and was at the Ternes address shown on the poster only from January to August of 1868. He did not do his own lettering; a pupil of his named Madaré handled this ably until his death in November 1894.

Offenbach, the son of the cantor of the Cologne synagogue, came to Paris as a youth. He played in the orchestra of the Opéra-Comique, managed several theaters and wrote more than 100 theatrical works, with which he established the traditions of French operetta. Le Château à Toto was one of three new works produced in 1868, another being La Périchole.

"Toto" is the nickname of Hector de la Roche-Trompette, a role created by Zulma Bouffar.

This is one of the earliest color lithograph posters in existence today. It is predominantly pale green, with the figures in a darker green and black. The large letters are white.

17. RAYON DES SOIERIES (Silk Department). Operetta; text by Nino; music by Manuel Rosenthal (born 1904). Opéra-Comique, June 2, 1930.
Poster by Maurice Dufrène; 46 x 31; printed by Chaix.

Dufrène also designed the sets and costumes for the operetta.

Rosenthal, a student of Ravel, was guest conductor, in May 1975, of the Ravel Festival of the New York State Ballet at Lincoln Center in New York. Composer of several operettas and other works, he also arranged the Offenbach pot-pourri for the ballet Gaîté Parisienne (1938).

In Rayon des Soieries, two young department store employees, their bosses and their customers are involved in a lively mixture of love and intrigue.

This, the most recent poster in the volume, is an example of the most distinctive style of the 1920s and 1930s, Art Deco (Art décoratif, which grew out of Cubism and Bauhaus, was first pulled together into one specific style most clearly in France). It is primarily in black, white and shades of gray, with a single fold of silk in pink and one in green.

18. PSYCHÉ. Opera; text by Jules Barbier and Michel Carré; music by Ambroise Thomas (1811–1896). Opéra-Comique, Jan. 26, 1857; new enlarged version, Opéra-Comique, May 21, 1878.
Poster with illustration by Antonin-Marie Chatinière; 34 x 24½; printed by Morris Père et Fils.

Thomas, a child prodigy on the piano and violin, entered the Paris Conservatoire at 17 and won many honors, including the Prix de Rome at age 21. At sixty, after a long, fruitful life as a composer, he succeeded Auber as director of the Conservatoire. He is best remembered today for his operas Mignon (1866) and Hamlet (1868). His new version of Psyché at the Opéra-Comique was given 24 performances during 1878, whereas the 1857 production, occurring in an unhappy period of the composer's life, had been a failure. See also Nos. 19 and 48.

The plot is based on the familiar story of Psyche and Cupid (here called Eros) as told by Apuleius. The poster shows the end of the opera; Eros, consoled by Mercury, grieves because

his kiss has proved fatal to his mortal wife, but Venus appears and restores their happiness.

The lettering is in dark blue on a pale blue ground. The illustration is in black and white. The recumbent figure of Psyche in the foreground bears a striking resemblance to that of Manon, by the same artist (Frontispiece).

19. LA TEMPÊTE (The Tempest). Ballet; scenario by Jules Barbier; music by Ambroise Thomas. Opéra, June 26, 1889.
Poster by E. Buval with an illustration by Bellenger; 32 x 23½; printed by Dupré.

Buval is one of the few artists I could find no information on at all. From the look of this poster and No. 20, with their great attention to lettering, I suspect he may have done title pages and covers for books and music.

This ballet, based on the Shakespeare play, was Thomas's last major composition. Hansen (1843–1927), a dancer and choreographer of the Royal Danish Ballet, was balletmaster of the Bolshoi Theater in Moscow from 1879 to 1889, working in Copenhagen and London during leaves from Russia. He was balletmaster of the Paris Opéra from 1890 to 1894. In La Tempête he danced the role of Caliban. Rosita Mauri, also the star of La Farandole (No. 4) and La Korrigane (No. 20), was born in Spain in 1856 and came to Paris in 1879 under the auspices of Gounod. She was the leading ballerina in Paris for two decades. In La Tempête she was Miranda.

The main body of the poster is in light blue with dark blue lettering; the title and ornamental scrolls are silver. The Bellenger illustration, a black-and-white engraving affixed to the poster, first appeared in the magazine L'Illustration. It depicts the final scene, in which, after the storm, a magnificent ship appears. At the bottom is a picture of Rosita Mauri.

20. LA KORRIGANE (The Goblin Maiden). Ballet; scenario by François Coppée and Louis Mérante; music by Charles-Marie Widor (1844–1937). Opéra, Dec. 1, 1880.
Poster by E. Buval; 32 x 23½; printed by Moucelot.

An outstanding organist (at Saint-Sulpice in Paris for over 60 years; teacher of Albert Schweitzer), Widor was also a distinguished composer (see also No. 52). La Korrigane, with a story by the eminent poet Coppée, was one of the most successful Opéra ballets. On Mérante, see No. 4. On Mauri, see No. 19.

The scene is mysterious Brittany, where the poor orphan Yvonnette vainly loves Lilez, the bagpiper. She needs fine clothes to win more than his pity and strikes a bargain with the Queen of the Korrigans (the malevolent spirits of Brittany), resulting in her being claimed as one of them. In the ballet's climax, the Queen says that the now ardent Lilez may have Yvonnette if he can single her out from the rest. He cannot, until she reprises the brilliant gigue bretonne she had done earlier. A friend of the lovers shows up with a sacred rosary just in time to save them from the wrath of the foiled Korrigans.

The poster shows the Act II setting of the heath and marsh with a menhir and dolmen; goblins and human beings (with the rosary) are visible. The insert shows Rosita Mauri doing the gigue bretonne. The illustrations are black, the lettering is orange and the ground is pale green.

21. CLAUDINE. Operetta; text by Willy; music by Rodolphe Berger. Théâtre du Moulin-Rouge, 1910.
Poster by Clérice Frères; 35 x 25½; printed by Ed. Delanchy.

On Berger, see No. 1.

Snails are creeping out of books while Claudine, brought to Paris by her preoccupied father (he is writing a scholarly work on snails), surveys the characters in the operetta.

The great French writer Colette began her career reluctantly.

Born Sidonie-Gabrielle Colette in 1873, at age 20 she married the music critic Henri Gauthier-Villars, called "Willy." At his instigation, and with considerable prodding, she adapted her diaries into the Claudine series, four novels published from 1900 to 1904. Although his contribution was small, the books appeared solely under the name "Willy," but it is interesting to note that Colette is credited as their co-author on this poster. Not until many years after her divorce in 1909 did she begin to sign her work with the single name Colette.

22. LOUISE. Opera; text and music by Gustave Charpentier (1860–1956). Opéra-Comique, Feb. 2, 1900.
    Poster by Georges Rochegrosse; 35½ x 24¾; printed by Ed. Delanchy & Cie.

Louise, although a great success, initiated no little controversy in its time. It is the story of a working-class girl who falls in love with a poet and goes to live with him, to the horror of her parents. They contrive to get her back, but their rigid values and drab existence are pitted against the bohemian life of Montmartre. Montmartre wins, Louise returns to her lover and the opera ends with her father shaking his fist at the city, crying mournfully, "Oh, Paris!"

Charpentier was lifted out of poverty by the success of *Louise*. He broke with operatic tradition in portraying the seamy side of contemporary life and his heroine was the symbol of a new freedom in the new century.

Mary Garden, an understudy at the Opéra-Comique, leapt to fame as Louise in Paris and made her American debut in the opera in 1908.

The poster shows us the third-act setting, with the two lovers tenderly embracing in their garden on the heights of Montmartre. Spread out below them, lights twinkling in the dusk, is the city some have called the real protagonist of the opera—Paris.

23. ANTAR. Opera; text by Chékri Ganem; music by Gabriel Dupont. Opéra, March 14, 1921.
    Poster by Georges Rochegrosse; 34¼ x 26; printed by Maquet.

On Dupont, see No. 6. *Antar* was in rehearsal at the Opéra in 1914, when the composer died at the age of 36 on the very day that war was declared. The performance was canceled and the opera was not given until nearly seven years later.

Antar was a sixth-century Arabian warrior-poet. In Arabian legend he is the embodiment of chivalry. In a review of Chékri Ganem's play, on which the opera is based, Adolphe Adérer (*Le Théâtre*) says we are indebted to *Antar* for wonderful phrases like: "It is only when husbands are present that I enter women's houses." Moralizing about his own society, he fears that now modern Arab poets, from associating with Europeans, give other advice, like: "When the husband is absent, one must eat of the fruits of the garden of love."

24. PÉNÉLOPE. Opera; text by René Fauchois; music by Gabriel Fauré (1845–1924). Monte Carlo, March 4, 1913.
    Poster by Georges Rochegrosse; 35½ x 27; printed by Maquet.

Fauré, a pupil of Saint-Saëns, became professor of composition at the Paris Conservatoire, where Ravel, Enesco and Nadia Boulanger were among his students. Many of his vocal and instrumental works have become standard concert pieces.

Pénélope, which had its Paris première at the Théâtre des Champs-Elysées on May 10, 1913, with Lucienne Bréval as Penelope and Lucien Muratore as Ulysses, tells the story of Ulysses' homecoming. Louis Schneider (*Le Théâtre*) called it "one of the most important events in French music for a long time" and praised Fauré for imitating only himself.

Note the hand at the bottom, dripping blood over the lettering

panel. The poster shows Ulysses and his loyal servants attacking Penelope's suitors. His figure is so forceful that it cannot be contained within the picture, but thrusts an arm beyond the top.

25. MONNA VANNA. Opera; text by Maurice Maeterlinck; music by Henry Février (1875–1957). Opéra, Jan. 13, 1909.
    Poster by Gustave Fraipont; 35 x 25; printed by Delanchy.

Fraipont was born in Brussels in 1849. He studied and lived in Paris and began to exhibit at the Salon des Artistes Français in 1896. The poster is signed by both Gustave and his son Georges (1873–1912).

Février, a pupil of Massenet and Fauré, wrote several operas, of which *Monna Vanna* was the most successful. The Belgian symbolist Maeterlinck based the libretto on his own well-known play of 1902.

Monna Vanna takes place in fifteenth-century Pisa, besieged by the Florentines. Vanna, the wife of Guido Colonna, the Pisan commander, transfers her love from her insanely jealous husband to the Florentine general Prinzivalle, and goes off with him after her city has been spared.

The poster represents a third-act grouping, set in the great hall of Colonna's palace: old Marco Colonna (Guido's father), Guido, Vanna and Prinzivalle.

26. CARMOSINE. Operetta; text by Henri Cain and Louis Payen; music by Henry Février. Théâtre Lyrique Municipal (Gaîté), Feb. 24, 1913.
    Poster by Vikke van den Bergh; 35¼ x 26¾; printed by R. Engelmann for R. Viellard.

Carmosine, the daughter of a rich doctor of Palermo, is affianced to Perillo, a law student. Alas, she sees her king at a tourney, falls madly in love with him and wants to die, for her love is hopeless. The king already has a queen, who counsels the girl to love her king, as indeed she should, but more purely. The king says tenderly that he will wear her colors at the next tourney, but that she must marry the young Perillo. Church bells sound and Carmosine awakes to marry Perillo happily, for it has all been a dream.

Henri de Curzon (*Le Théâtre*) compliments the librettists for their handling of this delicate tale, adapted from Boccaccio and Alfred de Musset. As for the music, he says it is "different and more respectable" than *Monna Vanna*, but is not struck by Février's originality.

The poster shows the King talking with Carmosine and Perillo in a night scene glowing with torchlight.

27. GISMONDA. Opera; text by Henri Cain and Louis Payen; music by Henry Février. Chicago, Jan. 14, 1919.
    Poster by Georges Rochegrosse; color lithograph; 36 x 27; printed by Maquet.

This libretto was adapted from the 1894 play which Victorien Sardou wrote for Sarah Bernhardt.

Gismonda, written in 1914 but held back by the war, was given its world première by Mary Garden's company in Chicago. After a New York hearing, it was performed at the Opéra-Comique on October 15, 1919, with Fanny Heldy in the title role. "The public seemed as enchanted as the music, the performers, the entire production," Henri de Curzon (*Le Théâtre*).

The poster, whose haunting blues intensify the tragedy of the scene, shows Gismonda (Act IV, Scene 1) about to kill the treacherous courtier Zacaria, who has plotted to kill her son and her lover.

28. LE RÊVE (The Dream). Ballet; scenario by Edouard Blau;

choreography by J. Hansen; music by Léon Gastinel (1823–1906). Opéra, June 9, 1890.

Poster by Théophile-Alexandre Steinlen; 35 x 25; printed by Gillot.

One of the most important graphic artists of his time, Steinlen (1859–1923) was born in Switzerland. In 1881 he came to Paris, where he lived humbly in Montmartre in a house full of the cats he loved to paint and that became his trademark. He was a Socialist, and although his posters seldom show the seamy side of life, his paintings and drawings were of the poor people of Paris: workers, vagrants, prostitutes. Anatole France called him "the master of the street." He did illustrations for books and magazines, notably *Gil Blas* and *Le Courrier Français*. The present poster, probably his earliest, shows Japanese influence, a major factor in the graphic art of the period.

Gastinel, a pupil of Halévy, won the Prix de Rome in 1846. Among his stage works were several operas and this ballet based on Japanese legend. J. Hansen (see No. 19) danced the role of the malevolent Sakouma. Rosita Mauri was the heroine Daïta.

The poster shows the giant fan in Act I that is opened by a magical arrow shot. At the top is the goddess Isanami, who leads the heroine behind the fan into a dream experience.

29. MAM'ZELLE BOY-SCOUT. Operetta; text by Paul Bonhomme; music by Gustave Goublier (d. 1926). Théâtre de la Renaissance, Apr. 3, 1915.

Poster by Henri Gray; 35 x 27; printed by Ed. Delanchy & Fils.

There has been much speculation about Gray's identity, but the catalogue of the Bibliothèque Nationale print department states definitely that Henri Gray (1858–1924) was a pseudonym of the Parisian caricaturist Boulanger, who also used the signature "Grivois" (spicy, racy) in illustrations for many magazines, including *Paris-Illustré* and *Paris S'Amuse*. In addition, he designed costumes for the Folies-Bergère. Maindron states that he was the subject of an article in *Le Courrier Français* in 1884.

The central figure of the poster, in high-heeled pumps, stands out in a good deal of space, while the artist has managed to include several incidents of the plot in light, detailed sketches.

30. LES TURCS (The Turks). Operetta; text by Hector Crémieux and A. Jaime; music by Hervé. Théâtre des Folies-Dramatiques, Dec. 23, 1869.

Poster by Jules Chéret; 29¾ x 22; printed by Chéret.

A scimitar and a pike weave through the title of this early poster, which was designed to tell a story rather than, as later in the art, to have a striking impact.

On Hervé, see No. 7.

Les Turcs is a parody of the seventeenth-century tragedy *Bajazet* by Jean Racine, which has a Turkish setting.

31. ESCLARMONDE. Opera; text by Alfred Blau and Louis de Gramont; music by Jules Massenet. Opéra-Comique, May 15, 1889.

Poster by Alfred Choubrac; 47 x 32½; printed by F. Appel, Paris and Lyons.

A student of Doerr and Pils, and a follower of Chéret, Alfred Choubrac (1853–1902) often worked with his brother Léon. The magazine *Chat Noir*, in 1883, honored Chéret and the Choubracs as masters of the poster. Maindron says that the first exhibition of illustrated posters, in 1884, was "certainly inspired by . . . Jules Chéret . . . and Léon and Alfred Choubrac." Léon used the signature "Hope," but both often left their works unsigned. Alfred once did a poster for the magazine *Fin de Siècle* that was recalled by the censors because of the scantily

clad female figure. Angered, he did another pull, this time whiting out the offending part and adding the words, "Cette partie du dessin a été interdite" (This part of the drawing has been forbidden).

On Massenet, see note on Frontispiece. See also Nos. 10–14 and 32–42.

Esclarmonde, taken from the old French romance *Partenopeus de Blois*, was a stunning spectacle for the huge audience brought to Paris for the Exposition of 1889. The title role was created for and by the beautiful American soprano Sybil Sanderson. Like *Cendrillon*, *La Navarraise*, *Le Cid* and *Don Quichotte*, *Esclarmonde* has recently enjoyed a revival.

The upper of the two small scenes shows the meeting of Esclarmonde and the French knight Roland on a magic island. The lower scene shows the siege of Blois in France, where Roland saves the king.

32. LE MAGE (The Magus). Opera; text by Jean Richepin; music by Jules Massenet. Opéra, Mar. 16, 1891.

Poster by Alfredo Edel; 35½ x 25¾; printed by Ch. Lévy.

Edel was born in Parma, Italy, in 1856 and died at Boulognesur-Seine in 1912. Chiefly a poster artist, he also designed the costumes for Massenet's *Chérubin* (see No. 39).

The Persian general Zarastra loves his Turanian captive, Queen Anahita, and does not return the love of Varedha, daughter of the high priest. Under constraint to marry Varedha, he chooses banishment and becomes a recluse, Le Mage. Though the Turanians attack again and burn the Persian capital, the lovers are reunited and Varedha dies, still cursing them. Rosita Mauri danced in the ballet scene.

The acid-tongued Willy (see *Claudine*) complained after the première: "It's very odd! When I hear Massenet's operas I always long for Saint-Saëns'. I should add that hearing Saint-Saëns' operas makes me long for Massenet's."

33. WERTHER. Opera; text by Edouard Blau, Paul Milliet and Georges Hartmann; music by Jules Massenet. Hofoper, Vienna, Feb. 16, 1892.

Poster, 1893, by Eugène Grasset; 31½ x 24; printed by Lemercier.

Grasset (1841–1917) was born in Lausanne and became a French citizen in 1891. He studied architecture, traveled to Egypt, then settled in Paris as a fabric designer. He founded a school of decorative art and designed stamps, book bindings, playing cards, typefaces, furniture and stained glass. The Heugel catalogue lists Grasset as the artist of this poster, but François Heugel suggests that while it was indeed designed and executed by him, the insert illustrations were probably taken from a former poster or book, artist unknown.

Based on Goethe's famous novel, *Werther* has remained one of Massenet's most popular operas, still in the current repertoire. Massenet, Milliet and the publisher Hartmann hit upon this choice of subject as early as 1880, while en route to Milan to have the Italian publisher Ricordi read the libretto of *Hérodiade* (see No. 11). The work was not ready for performance, however, until 1892, when it was given in German in Vienna. Acclaimed there, it was praised to the skies in Paris (Opéra-Comique, Jan. 16, 1893) by musicians, but less liked by the public. Brought back in 1903, however, it caught on.

The insert illustrations in the poster show Werther's dawning affection for Lotte, who marries another man, and his final declaration of love to her.

The librettist Paul Milliet wrote an article in *L'Art du Théâtre* (July 1903) about the history of this opera: "On returning [from the trip to Milan], I began to work and it is then that my troubles began. For four years . . . I polished and repolished without end, introducing an episode one day that failed to survive the next and saw the light again the day after, not because of Massenet (I hardly saw my collaborator) but according to the whim of the publisher [note Hartmann's credit as librettist]. It was because of all those cuts and arbitrary additions that my friend Edouard Blau became my collaborator."

34. THAÏS. Opera; text by Louis Gallet; music by Jules Massenet. Opéra, Mar. 16, 1894.
Poster by Manuel Orazi; 42 x 15; printed by Lemercier.

The opera, based on Anatole France's novel, takes place in early Christian Egypt. The cenobite Athanaël converts the courtesan Thaïs and persuades her to leave sinful Alexandria. As she lies ill in her desert convent, he comes and confesses that he feels carnal love for her, but she dies in true repentance and sanctity. The original Thaïs in Paris was Sybil Sanderson; Mary Garden was the first to sing the role in America (Manhattan Opera House, 1907), Geraldine Farrar the first at the Metropolitan (1917).

Maindron (Les Affiches Illustrées) describes this poster as resembling "a papyrus, torn, eaten away by the centuries. M. Orazi has created for Massenet's Thaïs a poster that is the first to have such a curious form." The artist's distinctive signature appears in a red circle to the right of the monk's foot.

35. CENDRILLON (Cinderella). Opera, text by Henri Cain; music by Jules Massenet. Opéra-Comique, May 24, 1899.
Poster by Emile Bertrand; 31¼ x 23½; printed by Devambez.

The catalogue of the Bibliothèque de l'Opéra attributes this Art Nouveau poster to the printer Devambez (note his signature at the lower left, in addition to the name of his firm at the lower right), but the original Heugel catalogue lists Emile Bertrand as the artist. Bertrand, a painter and engraver, was an exhibiting member of the Salon des Artistes Français.

The plot of Cendrillon is a greatly expanded version of the traditional fairy tale. It was the first of several Massenet works created at the Opéra-Comique during the régime of its great director Albert Carré.

Twenty-four pages of Le Théâtre, July 1899, were given entirely to Cendrillon, which Louis Schneider called "a treat for the eye as well as the ear." He made the somewhat puzzling comment that the librettist, Henri Cain, had an unnamed collaborator, the painter Paul Collin [sic]. As for Carré, Schneider said that with Cendrillon he was able for the first time to "give the full measure of his capabilities."

36. GRISÉLIDIS. Opera; text by Armand Silvestre and Eugène Morand; music by Jules Massenet. Opéra-Comique, Nov. 20, 1901.
Poster by François Flameng; 54½ x 30½; printed by Bourgerie & Cie.

Flameng (1859–1923), a pupil of Cabanel, Laurens, Hédouin and his father Léon, exhibited at the Salon de Paris from 1875, and won the Grand Prix in 1889. A popular artist, he did portraits of French officials.

Massenet had seen the play Grisélidis at the Comédie Française in the early 1890s and had asked the authors to transform it into an opera libretto.

The story is the legend of Griselda, adapted from the Decameron of Boccaccio. The Marquis Gaultier falls in love with a beautiful lower-class woman and marries her. He is so sure of her that he accepts the Devil's proposition to test her fidelity. In Boccaccio, Griselda's husband mistreats her; in the opera, the Devil tempts her. She withstands every temptation and all ends well.

Lucienne Bréval of the Opéra came to the Opéra-Comique to sing the title role. The baritone Hector Dufranne as the Marquis

was the revelation of the evening.

In his review, Adolphe Jullien speaks of Grisélidis as "a magnificent spectacle in its entirety." He goes on to compliment the sixty-year-old Massenet for continuing to charm audiences with fresh melodies, unspoiled by too heavy and violent instrumentation. In another rave review the director, Albert Carré, was called "a magician."

37. CIGALE. Ballet; scenario by Henri Cain; music by Jules Massenet. Opéra-Comique, Feb. 4, 1904.
Poster by Maurice Leloir; 35 x 22; printed by Devambez.

Leloir (1853–1940) did historical paintings and theater designs, and wrote a history of French costume. He was technical adviser on films (especially those based on Dumas) for Douglas Fairbanks, Sr., receiving credit as production designer on The Iron Mask, 1929.

This ballet, based on La Fontaine's fable "La Cigale et la Fourmi" (The Cicada [usually referred to as Grasshopper] and the Ant), was originally performed at a benefit evening on behalf of the Opéra-Comique orchestra, chorus and stage crew.

Generous Cigale gives away all her worldly goods to her friend La Pauvrette, while thrifty Mme. Fourmi laughs at her. When she later begs to be let in from the cold, Mme. Fourmi refuses, sneering, "Dance now, why don't you?" Cigale then sees La Pauvrette and her own Petit Ami in amorous embrace. In sorrow, she lets herself die of cold in the snow while angels surround her.

The poster is so cold that even the letters of the title are covered with snow.

38. LE JONGLEUR DE NOTRE-DAME (The Juggler of Our Lady). Opera; text by Maurice Léna; music by Jules Massenet. Monte Carlo, Feb. 18, 1902.
Poster, 1904, by Georges Rochegrosse; 35½ x 25½; printed by E. Delanchy.

Léna was a professor of philosophy at Lyons who submitted his unsolicited libretto to Massenet. The composer, captivated by the medieval legend, began setting it at once. First performed in Monte Carlo in 1902, the work came to the Opéra-Comique on May 10, 1904. Originally there were no female roles, but a few years later Mary Garden persuaded Massenet to adapt the tenor role of Jean, the Juggler, for her.

On the first of May, the feast of the Virgin Mary, a poor, emaciated juggler appears among the dancers near the famous abbey of Cluny. Invited to the abbey, where all the monks are preparing gifts for the Virgin, all he can offer is his juggling and his worldly songs and dances. The monks are horrified, but the image of the Virgin comes to life and blesses him. He dies in ecstasy, while the Prior cries: "Happy are the simple, for they will see God."

The lettering of this poster is "hung" on a wrought-iron sign and becomes part of the scene: the final moments of the opera in the abbey chapel.

39. CHÉRUBIN. Opera; text by Francis de Croisset and Henri Cain; music by Jules Massenet. Monte Carlo, Feb. 14, 1905.
Poster by Maurice Leloir; 35 x 25; printed by Devambez.

This opera was performed at the Opéra-Comique on May 23, 1905, shortly after its Monte Carlo première, with Mary Garden in the title role at both. The costumes were designed by Alfredo Edel (see No. 32).

Chérubin (inspired by Beaumarchais's character in Le Mariage de Figaro) is a young page who has many loves. He marries Nina, the girl he loves most, but still has the soul of a Don Juan.

Cupid, lying in the C of the title, seems to be laughing at

what he is about to do. Leloir has filled the poster with romantic props—ribbons, scrolls, flowers, a lute—and has used the cherub's dress-up scarf as a backdrop for the composer's name.

40. ARIANE (Ariadne). Opera; text by Catulle Mendès; music by Jules Massenet. Opéra, Oct. 31, 1906.
Poster by Albert Maignan; 35½ x 25½; printed by Devambez.

Maignan (1845–1908), born at Beaumont-le-Vicomte, made many trips tō Venice. *Ariane* is typical of his historical paintings, which he began to show at the Salon de Paris in 1868; they can now be seen in many French museums, including those of Angers and Lille.

The Greek legend of Theseus' abandonment of the Cretan princess Ariadne on the island of Naxos after she helped him to destroy the Minotaur has served as the basis of at least forty operas and poems. On the opening night of Massenet's work, Lucienne Bréval was Ariane, Lucy Arbell (see No. 41) was Perséphonc, and Lucien Muratore made his Opéra debut as Thésée.

Maignan used the device of an insert to add content to his poster, then let Ariadne's robe spill over the decoration at the bottom, somehow combining all into a beautifully integrated design.

James Harding (*Massenet*) reports that although Massenet praised his librettist to the skies, the composer "very often meant the exact opposite of what he said. The fact is that he and Catulle Mendès detested each other."

41. DON QUICHOTTE (Don Quixote). Opera; text by Henri Cain; music by Jules Massenet. Monte Carlo, Feb. 19, 1910.
Poster by Georges Rochegrosse; 35¼ x 27; printed by Ed. Delanchy.

The first Paris performance, at the Théâtre Lyrique Municipal (Gaîte), took place on December 29, 1910, ten months after the Monte Carlo première.

Jacques Le Lorrain, author of *Le Chevalier de la Longue Figure*, the Don Quixote play on which this opera was based, died only a few days after his play was first performed in 1904. Raoul Gunsbourg, director of the Monte Carlo Opera, recommended the play to Massenet as an operatic subject. Chaliapin sang the title role at Monte Carlo. The first Dulcinée at Monte Carlo and in Paris was Lucy Arbell (née Georgette Wallace), Massenet's last love, who was the first to portray at least six of his heroines. He became angry at her toward the end of his life. There was a good deal of rancor between her and his family, and after his death her lawsuits delayed performances of his last works.

Louis Schneider praised Massenet for this opera because instead of using the leitmotif, "so much abused since Wagner, he clothes his characters in harmonious individualities"; he added that *Don Quichotte* belonged "among the greatest successes of the master."

The blue hills and colorful sky in this poster are particularly striking examples of the intense crayon-like character of lithography.

42. PANURGE. Opera; text by Georges Spitzmüller and Maurice Boukay; music by Jules Massenet. Théâtre Lyrique Municipal (Gaîte), Apr. 25, 1913.
Poster by Charles-Lucien Léandre; 35½ x 24½; printed by J. Minot.

The artist Léandre (1862–1934), born in Normandy, began his career in Paris painting decorative pictures for hotels, then studied at the Beaux-Arts with Cabanel. He won many honors and was active in such artists' organizations as the Société des Peintres-Lithographes. He lived and worked in Montmartre among his friends Willette, Caran d'Ache and de Feure, who, along with Signac, Pissarro, Vallotton, Steinlen and other left-wing artists, did illustrations for anarchist journals. Léandre was known for his caricatures, many of which he drew for the periodical *Le Rire*. A street in Montmartre bears his name and a statue of him was erected in Paris after his death.

Panurge, based on characters and situations in Rabelais's *Pantagruel*, had its première eight months after Massenet's death. The role of Panurge was sung by Vanni Marcoux, that of his wife Colombe by Lucy Arbell. This was Arbell's final role in a Massenet opera (see No. 14).

43. VIVIANE. Ballet; scenario by Edmond Gondinet; music by Raoul Pugno (1852–1914) and Clément Lippacher. Eden-Théâtre, Oct. 28, 1886.
Poster by Jules Chéret; 31 x 23¾; printed by the Chéret branch of Chaix.

Pugno, a celebrated piano virtuoso and student of Thomas, died while on a concert tour in Moscow. He wrote several theater pieces, including this ballet (with Lippacher) in which Viviane, Lancelot, Merlin and Morgana dance amid veils and magic to spin out the Arthurian legend.

The druidess Viviane possesses magic powers only when she is in love and is loved in return, but her sweetheart Maël becomes entangled with the amorous Queen Guinevere.

The poster, more striking than earlier Chéret works, is more characteristic of his later designs. It features one of Chéret's typical girls ("Chérettes," as they were called by admiring Parisians)—frothy, lovely, alluring yet chaste—a style in girls, art, theater, music, everything, that was immensely popular in the Belle Epoque.

44. LES FÊTARDS (The Playboys). Operetta; text by Antony Mars and Maurice Hennequin; music by Victor Roger (1854–1903). Théâtre du Palais-Royal, Oct. 28, 1897.
Poster after Pal (Jean de Paléologue); 31½ x 23½; printed by E. Delanchy.

Pal, born in Bucharest in 1855, studied and worked in Paris. He did many bicycle posters, his specialty being voluptuous women like the lovely brunette in pink for *Les Fêtards*. He once did a poster to advertise the seaside resort of Cabourg that Maindron says must have led hordes there, particularly if the model, "as pleasingly undressed as the copy," went along too.

This was one of the more successful of the thirty or so theatrical works that Roger composed. *Les Fêtards* was essentially a farce with song and dance numbers, taking place in Biarritz and Paris. The text by Mars and Hennequin, a popular comedy-writing team, was adapted for a Broadway musical in 1899, *The Rounders*, with a new score by Ludwig Englander.

Apparently the poster had to be reprinted after the original lithographic stone had been scraped for reuse, for this is a second-edition lithograph drawn after (*d'après*) Pal.

45. LA REINE INDIGO (Queen Indigo). Operetta; French text by A. Jaime and Victor Wilder; music by Johann Strauss II (1825–1899). Théâtre de la Renaissance, Apr. 27, 1875.
Poster by Jules Chéret; 30 x 22; printed by Chéret.

This was the first French production of Strauss's first operetta with Zulma Bouffar as the heroine, Fantasca. In its original German (text by Maximilian Steiner), *Indigo und die vierzig Räuber* (Indigo and the Forty Thieves) was first performed in Vienna on Feb. 10, 1871. The story is based on *Arabian Nights* motifs, and Strauss derived his popular "1001 Nights Waltz" from musical themes composed for *Indigo*.

Feet seem to be dancing on the name of the composer, who, the poster proudly proclaims, is "from Vienna."

46. LA TZIGANE (The Gypsy Girl). Operetta; text by Alfred Delacour and Victor Wilder; music by Johann Strauss II. Théâtre de la Renaissance, Oct. 30, 1877.

Poster by Jules Chéret; 31 x 23½; printed by Chéret.

Having failed to get Meilhac and Halévy to adapt *Le Réveillon* (see No. 47), Strauss had Delacour and Wilder write an entirely different French book to the (practically uncut) *Fledermaus* score.

This short-lived French production of 1877, seldom mentioned in lists of Strauss's work, had a Hungarian setting. A young prince runs away on the eve of his wedding without ever having seen his fiancée. Later, when a band of Gypsies is gathered at an inn, the abandoned bride joins the troupe in disguise and is proclaimed their queen. Of course, the prince falls in love with her and complications ensue, but all is resolved happily.

47. LA CHAUVE-SOURIS (Die Fledermaus; The Bat). Operetta; French text by Paul Ferrier; music by Johann Strauss II. Théâtre des Variétés, Apr. 22, 1904.

Poster by Georges Dola; 31½ x 23½; printed by Ch. Wall et Cⁱᵉ (Atelier Dola).

Dola was born in 1872 at Dôle in eastern France. He had his own studio in Paris, and for a time worked with Jacques Wély (see No. 50).

Strauss never saw *La Chauve-Souris*, for although he had first tried to get the libretto done in 1872, it was not until 1904, when he had been dead five years, that it saw the light in Paris. Henri de Curzon (*Le Théâtre*, May 1904) tells the story: "In 1872, at the Palais-Royal, a light but nevertheless profound comedy by Meilhac and Halévy, *Le Réveillon*, began its successful run. Strauss loved it and begged the authors to adapt it for him. They refused, possibly because had they done it at all, it would have been for their preferred composer, Offenbach. Strauss then went to Haffner and Genée for a German libretto. They modified the French play very little and on April 5, 1874 Vienna furiously applauded the triumphant *Fledermaus*." After telling about *La Tzigane* (see No. 46), de Curzon continues: "Now, almost 30 years later, Strauss having died, the director of the Variétés has persuaded a more indulgent Halévy [Meilhac, too, was dead] to give Paul Ferrier permission to make the French adaptation."

The poster shows Prince Orloffsky's ball in the second act.

48. FRANÇOISE DE RIMINI. Opera; text by Jules Barbier and Michel Carré; music by Ambroise Thomas. Opéra, Apr. 14, 1882.

Poster by Jules Chéret; 30½ x 21¾; printed by the Chéret branch of Chaix.

On Thomas, see Nos. 18 and 19. *Françoise de Rimini*, completed when he was 71, was his most important composition after assuming directorship of the Paris Conservatoire in 1871. The busy librettists, Barbier and Carré, are best known for their text to Gounod's *Faust* (1859).

The plot is based on the Paolo and Francesca episode in the fifth canto of Dante's *Inferno*, which has inspired numerous plays and musical works. Françoise, for reasons of state, must marry the ugly deformed son of Malatesta. She is tricked into believing her groom will be another son, Paul, with whom she is already in love. Despite the marriage, Françoise and Paul cannot deny their love, and a third brother, jealous, betrays them to Françoise's husband, who kills them both.

The upper part of the poster shows the lovers as viewed by Dante, whom Vergil is guiding through the underworld (the underworld is the actual locale of the prologue and epilogue of the opera). The lower part shows Françoise's husband about to kill her and Paul.

49. LE PAPA DE FRANCINE. Operetta; text by Victor de Cottens and Paul Gavault; music by Louis Varney (1844–1908). Théâtre Cluny, Nov. 5, 1896.

Poster by Alfred Choubrac (?); 31½ x 23¾; printed by E. Delanchy.

Although the publisher's catalogue credits the printer Appel as the creator of this unsigned poster, it is difficult to believe that the actual artist was not Alfred Choubrac (see No. 31), who regularly used Appel's shop. The faces and figures are certainly in the style of his lighter work.

Varney was born in New Orleans, where his father was directing a French opera company, but spent most of his life in Paris. He wrote more than 35 operettas, most of which were successful in their time.

In *Le Papa de Francine*, the heroine searches for her father and finds him, at the same time winning Bob, her English teacher, who has taught her only the most important phrases, like "I love you" and "Kiss me."

50. LES DEMOISELLES DES SAINT-CYRIENS. Operetta; text by Paul Gavault and Victor de Cottens; music by Louis Varney. Théâtre Cluny, Jan. 22, 1898.

Poster by Jacques Wély; 31½ x 23½; printed by Ed. Delanchy et Cⁱᵉ (Ateliers J. Wély et G. Dola).

Wély (ca. 1873–1910) was a painter, lithographer and book illustrator.

A girls' boarding school is conveniently located near the aristocratic officers' training school, Saint-Cyr. In the risqué plot typical of French operettas of the time, the heroine is not only involved romantically with a cadet, but is also faced with the prospect of an inheritance—provided she competes in a nude beauty contest.

51. LE FIANCÉ DE THYLDA. Operetta; text by Victor de Cottens and Robert Charvay; music by Louis Varney. Théâtre Cluny, Jan. 26, 1900.

Poster by René Péan; 33 x 23; printed by Chaix (Ateliers Chéret).

Péan, a student of Chéret, worked in his studio and later went on to stage designing.

The scene is Stockholm. Thylda's fiancé is Otto, and her father is the same Baron von Gondremarck who appeared as a young man in Offenbach's *La Vie Parisienne* (1866). The baron decides that before the wedding his future son-in-law should have the same opportunity for adventures in Paris that he had. He sends him off but Thylda makes him miss his train. He goes anyway . . . in a dream. On awakening, he finds that the dream has sufficed and is content to confine his travels to a honeymoon trip.

Adolphe Adérer (*Le Théâtre*) stated: "This work shows that the operetta is not as sick as people say. No genre dies if it is done well. The good ones are as successful as the good operettas of the past." He concluded: "M. Varney's music is easy, abundant and certain to become popular as well as to appeal to more delicate ears."

52. LES PÊCHEURS DE SAINT-JEAN (The Fishermen of Saint-Jean-de-Luz). Opera; text by Henri Cain; music by Charles-Marie Widor. Opéra-Comique, Dec. 26, 1905.

Poster, 1906, by Fernand-Louis Gottlob; 35½ x 25½; printed by Delanchy (Atelier F. Gottlob).

Gottlob (1873–1935), who was born and died in Paris, led a double life artistically, as did so many poster artists. He painted street scenes of Paris and Brittany and, starting in 1891, exhibited many times at the Salon de Paris. Equally, he did humorous drawings for magazines like *Le Rire, L'Assiette au Beurre* and *Gil Blas*.

On Widor, see No. 20. Widor, who was born in Lyons and lived in Paris, made several trips to the Basque coast to imbibe atmosphere for *Les Pêcheurs*, his most successful opera.

In this starkly tragic story of ocean storm and implacable hatred, a penniless pilot loves the beautiful daughter of a prosperous boat owner, and is accepted by her father only after he saves the lives of some shipwrecked people.

Louis Schneider (*Le Théâtre*) called Widor's music strong and well-balanced: "the orchestration is solid without the bizarre qualities which certain people use in order to make themselves seem original." He praised Carré's direction and had only good to say of the entire Opéra-Comique production.